Sounding
the
Shofar
Why, When, Where

Call Upon Him
Jeremiah 33:3

Review
Protocol
Techniques
Scriptures

Learn
Psalm 47

Janet Rae Askins
Shofar Psalmist

WESTBOW
P R E S S®
A DIVISION OF THOMAS NELSON
& ZONDERVAN

WestBow Press books may be ordered through booksellers or by contacting:

WestBow Press
A Division of Thomas Nelson & Zondervan
1663 Liberty Drive
Bloomington, IN 47403
www.westbowpress.com
1 (866) 928-1240

ISBN: 978-1-5127-5598-5 (sc)
ISBN: 978-1-5127-5599-2 (e)

Print information available on the last page.

WestBow Press rev. date: 10/27/2016

CONTENTS

Foreword... ix

Section 1

Foreword... 1
What the Shofar is Not... 3
Despise not Small Beginnings... 8
An Interrogation Instrument... 10
Who Blew?.. 15
Citing Writings.. 21
Conclusion.. 31
The Shofarist Synopsis... 35

Section 2
Shofar Notes

Foreword... 37
Introduction... 38
Signaling the Seasons... 40
Shofar – Notes... 42
Words of Advice... 44
So You want to be a Shofar Sower?...................................... 46
Sounds... 51
Sacrificial Sound... 53
God Gravitator... 54
Going from Frozen to Chosen... 58
Would you like to know How to Embarrass Yourself? 60
Usher in the Holy Spirit... 62

When you are the Shofar Chauffeur...65

Hunting a Horn 69

Homework Assignment 73

Products 74

About the Author...75

Janet Rae Askins

Dedicates this writing to

<u>HONOR</u>

GOD THE FATHER:
Who became real to me at age 3 when HE draped a mantel
of unconditional love (a down comforter to the mind of a
3 year old – maybe it was filled with Angel feathers!).

WHERE
In the musty basement of Travis Park Methodist
Church, San Antonio, Texas.

THE SON:
Who appeared to me as a teenager during summer camp vespers.

WHERE
At Mount Wesley Church Camp in Kerrville, Texas.

THE HOLY SPIRIT:
Who zapped me with a bolt of SPIRITUAL lightening
that came through my uplifted hand and went out
my right big toe during the church service.

WHERE
May 9, 1976
At First Baptist Church in Lubbock, Texas

This writing is a special LOVE GIFT to God's people (that's **YOU**).

Thank you my precious daughters - Carolin Renee for your love and
dedication in editing this booklet and to Marilyn Janae (whom I was
dedicating to the Lord when HE got my attention on May 9, 1976)
for all your love and encouragement. I am so blessed to have these
daughters, their spouses, and 6 grandchildren in my life.

FOREWORD

Shofar Sow Good is intriguing as it's title and is literally a "string of pearls;" a "basket of lovely nuggets." Isn't it just like God to select as His instrument one so simple, without valves, strings, keys, pads, springs, slide, reed, bow, bell or whistle!

After reading Janet's epistle to the Shofar, the next time through your King James, you will sense that the scales have literally fallen from your eyes.

The meat in this banquet of gems is great excitement for both babe and scholar.

You will not be satisfied to read this beautiful panoply just once because you will marvel at how you missed so much in the pure Word whether you are a first or fiftieth timer.

Janet Rae Askins is a 21st Century Esther wielding her Shofar/scepter; precious to the Lord and the Body of Christ.

Dennis G. Brewer, Sr.
BBA, LLB, Dr. of Laws, Bible Teacher

Section 1

FOREWORD

"Why do you carry around an animal horn?" is the question often asked of me. Simply put, the Lord asked me to carry it along with my Bible, and I've noticed He uses foolish things to confound the wise! The SHOFAR is a voice in the wilderness of today's dry and barren land. People have so much knowledge of God, but do not seem to know how to get in touch with God. I've noticed this piercing sound helps usher people into His presence.

On a trip to Oxford, England to visit my sister Linda, I stood in the parking lot of the airport and took a deep breath of fresh country air. Oh how I had forgotten what it was like to experience unpolluted air!!! Likewise, in spiritual terms, the doctrines of men, the atmosphere of rejection & pain, and the hustle/hassle of life have so clouded our minds, that we are sometimes unable to tap into His domain and receive the refreshing we need.

These writings are the result of my personal research and finding little practical information on the SHOFAR. So many friends have asked me to write my findings, and while it may not be a complete work, it is an attempt to help satisfy some of the questions people have asked.

What spine tingling, toe curling sound cuts open your innermost spirit like a physician's scalpel to reveal what is present? The voice of the SHOFAR or SHOPHAR. Let's explore the history and discover why this almost forgotten instrument is being introduced back into the church to usher in the glory of God.

Have we become so sophisticated that we choose to totally ignore what might be considered God's favorite instrument?

HE will be sounding the SHOFAR to call His bride, His beloved to her new home. Will you recognize the cry "COME"? For no man knows the day or the hour of His call for you as an individual *** ARE YOU READY?

WHAT THE SHOFAR IS NOT

THOU SHALT HAVE NO OTHER GODS BEFORE ME *Exodus 20:3*

While coming out of a deep sleep one morning these words penetrated my mind. They were fresh off the heavenly press and delivered to me by the Holy Spirit.

"The SHOFAR is NOT a magical charm or a tinker toy – honor the office of the SHOFAR."

My whole body was paralyzed with the fear of the Lord, for I KNEW –

HE HAD SPOKEN.

I BEGAN QUIVERING ALL OVER AND MY HEART RACED.

"What are you saying, Lord?"

There was no reply, but I instantly KNEW it was my responsibility to educate, warn, and encourage the body of Christ to be careful how they handle this new wave of SHOFAR blowing. The SHOFAR is NOT to be taken lightly and used as another gimmick to excite the people. It is to be regarded as an instrument to blast open an invisible shaft and usher the hearer into the very presence of God whereby they can communicate with the King of the Universe for themselves!

Proverbs 9:10 The fear of the Lord is the beginning of wisdom; and the knowledge of the holy is understanding.

Now that we have an understanding of what the SHOFAR is NOT, we can study what it **IS**:

WHY THE CRY OF THE SHOFAR?

THE SHOFAR HAS A CLARION CALL THAT REQUESTS A RESPONSE, EITHER FROM THE HEARER OR FROM GOD, A TYPE OF RSVP.

YAWEH - Hebrew for God - so highly esteemed the SHOFAR, also known as the Ram's Horn, that HE set aside an entire day of rest and reflection, for the Blowing of the Trumpets, or the Feast of Trumpets. (Leviticus 23:24 and Numbers 29:1) This day is known as Rash Hashanah, the Jewish New Year, celebrating the creation of earth, and is also referred to as Yom Teru'ah or the head of the year.

In my Hebrew class we learned that "feast" referred to a word that meant a solemn assembly, a celebration, or a rehearsal of things to come; therefore, we can be reminded that the Feast of Trumpets is a foretaste of the happenings that will take place in heaven - on earth as it is in Heaven. Leviticus 23:24 states " ... *a Sabbath, a memorial of blowing of trumpets, and holy convocation.*" Convocation, according to Strong's #4744, means assembly and rehearsal. God went on to say in verse 31, "... *it shall be a statute forever throughout your generations in all your dwellings.*" HE repeated this command in Numbers 29:1 " ...*ye shall do no servile work: it is a day of blowing the trumpets unto you.*" We learned when God repeats Himself; you'd better sit up and pay attention!!!

The following pages are designed to provide a passageway to rediscover the purposes and power of this God made instrument of authority. May you be inspired and edified while you learn why the SHOFAR is being introduced back into the church. It's used as a voice in worship to prepare the congregation's hearts to receive God's word. It also serves as an effective weapon to confuse and command the enemy to depart.

We didn't do away with baptism and communion because they are old commandments. Why then are we not still in compliance with the law of the blowing of the SHOFAR? Shouldn't we reinstate this somewhat forgotten instrument of the Priests? I can find where "God said" and "God commanded" when referring to blowing the trumpet, but cannot find one place where God says, "and you shall no longer need to blow the trumpet."

The Talmud, the Jewish Book of Law, says, "When there's judgment from below, there's no need for judgment from above."

If you picture in your mind a courtroom scene, you can think of the SHOFAR as the call to order, "All arise, the honorable Judge of the Universe is now presiding". We need to request HE now move from the Seat of Judgment to the Seat of Mercy. We will ALL stand before HIM to be judged. There is a knowing someone else is holding your future.

Many times before the SHOFAR is blown, a quote is spoken:

"Blessed are you, Lord our God, Ruler of the Universe, who sanctifies us by your commandments and commands us to hear the SHOFAR. Praised are you, Lord our God, the Ruler of the Universe, who has kept us in life and enabled us to reach this season."

LET THE CELEBRATION BEGIN!!!

Blessed is the people that know the joyful sound. Psalm 89:15

Strong's Concordance # 8643 explains joyful "sound" in this isolated Biblical usage: "An acclamation of joy, a battle cry, clangor of trumpets, jubilee, and rejoicing."

In Hebrew the phrase is:

ASHREI HA-AM YODEl T'RUAH
Blessed (is) the people (who) know the SHOFAR blast.

5

Note the T'ruah is one of the official blasts that is the staccato sounds of the SHOFAR.

A VOICE OF CHOICE

What sends chills down your spine and tingles in your toes?
What frightens the devil and increases his woes?
What IS that sound ** causing the enemy to flee?
Why it's the SHOFAR voice *** that appeals to me!
From Heaven to Hell you can hear that cry

therefore;

NOW IS THE TIME TO DETERMINE WHY
You should spend your days in serving the Lord
In admiration and praise - He is to be adored!
Examine yourself, and surely you'll find
You are glad *** that HE is so kind!

Have you taken out time to look and see
WHO is coming back
for YOU and me?

GGG

WHERE IS "HOME"

My former pastor, Dr. Clara Reed, brought an encouraging and thought provoking sermon on anticipating going to heaven beginning with, "Have you ever been homesick?" There's a gnawing to reconnect with the familiar – the sights, sounds, smells, and experiences where you have been comfortable, loved, and accepted."

When you hear the SHOFAR for the very first time, it almost seems familiar, like a voice from heaven calling you home. It's as if the battle is already over and the victory has been proclaimed. There is an unspeakable joy that wells up on your inside and you instinctively know the very mind and heart of the Messiah calling His BRIDE. (That's you!!!)

God desires for everyone to reach HIS HOME, but why will so many miss the opportunity? Dennis Lindsay stated in our Creation Science class at Christ For The Nations that many people say, "I want to be God so I can make up my own rules." They are too proud to recognize they need a Savoir.

DESPISE NOT SMALL BEGINNINGS

Do you know that one seemingly small event in your life can chart the entire course of your future?

In 1956, my mother and I walked up some worn stone steps in an old Catholic School in San Antonio, Texas and down the long narrow corridor to a vacated classroom. It was there {memorialize the THERE'S in your life} a band director, M. E. Rodman, who was giving private lessons looked at Mother and said, "she needs to play the French Horn." He brought out this enormous (from the eyes of a 12 year old) instrument and said, "Blow as loud as you can." To both our surprise, a marvelous sound came forth! TODAY, I realize this was God's provision for me to "pierce the darkness in my life" and give ole Satan a bellyache! (My testimony will be in another book). You see, the *French Horn is actually the man-made modern version of the Biblical SHOFAR.* There were private lessons, practicing, state band, state orchestra, college music scholarship, and other opportunities that followed, but none of those honors could get me into heaven's gate. I can truthfully say that without the love for the music that soothed my soul and my dedication to playing this horn, I would not be alive. If I would have known that all the while God was preparing me to play HIS instrument of deliverance, I would have practiced a lot more!!!

When you review what you thought about and loved as a child, you might discover secret passageways to your future!

Proverbs 29:18 (Ber version) *"Where there is no vision the people run wild: but happy is he who keeps the law."* Do you know some unhappy, unruly people? Perhaps they have not discovered their secret passageway and have no vision of who they are in God's eyes - are YOU the one God has assigned to nurture and mentor them?

AN INTERROGATION INSTRUMENT

The SHOFAR is known as probably the only instrument that requires a response. In these pages, you will notice many questions. It is a Hebrew custom to answer a question with a question; therefore the author would like to stimulate your thinking patterns to help you say, "Yes, Lord, here am I. What would you ask me to do? To think? To pray? To be? Your servant heareth and will obey." I don't believe anyone can fully experience HIS marvelous overwhelming JOY until you are in the right relationship with HIM.

FEATURING FASCINATING FACTS

The SHOFAR may have been the very first instrument on earth and sometimes referred to as the Jubal or Yobel Horn. In Strong's #3104 the Hebrew Yobel goes back to Jubal who was the father of all instruments in Genesis 4:21 and where we get our word Jubilee or freedom. *Leviticus 25:9-10* commands the trumpet of the Jubilee to sound throughout the land on the day of taking away of sin and every 50th year to proclaim freedom - thus we see the inscription of the U.S. Liberty Bell - *PROCLAIM LIBERTY THROUGHOUT THE LAND UNTO ALL THE INHABITANTS THEREOF.*

Strong's #8231, SHAPHAR means to glisten, to make fair, beauty, referring to GLORY. It's interesting that one of the most popular SHOFAR is made from the KUDU antelope. Webster's uses the word kudos, plural, for GLORY when we want to honor someone. LET US GIVE GLORY TO THE FATHER, SON, AND HOLY SPIRIT WITH THIS GOD MADE INSTRUMENT!!!

Another root word found in Strong's #7782, SHOPHAR, means cutting and incising, or making a clear sound. Webster's describes incision as the act of cutting into or engraving something, a thin cut, especially one made by a scalpel in surgery; to close an incision with stitches. Something to ponder here is HE came to touch our infirmities and heal our wounds.

In the plural form, TRUMPETS according to Strong's #2689 & 2690 means to surround with a stockade and thus separate from the open country.

Trumpet in the New Testament Greek is Strong's #4536 meaning through the idea of quavering or reverberation, and in #4537, to trumpet, sound a blast (which are yet to) sound. These mostly refer to future events.

The modem day version of the SHOFAR. the French Horn, is made out of a 16 foot (5-meter) piece of brass whereas the "Ram's Horn" can be as small as 6" with a slight curve to the very large 2, 3, or 4 twists and up to 54" or more in length depending on the animal that was sacrificed.

According to Jewish law, this God made instrument can be fashioned out of the horns of any kosher animal such as the sheep, goat, mountain goat, antelope or gazelle. It cannot be made from a cow's horn because it is considered an unclean animal and it is reminiscent of the golden calf that Aaron constructed and worshiped as an idol in the desert. The Rabbis believe if an unclean animal horn was used that Satan would be reminded to continue to accuse Israel for this incident and God would deal harshly when judging them. It's interesting that the Kudu antelope (that grows the horns fashioned into SHOFARS I use most often) is considered to have the most sensitive ears and is the very animal that warns all the other animals in the jungle when danger is near with a barking sound.

The SHOFAR carried the anointing oil in which to anoint kings. I Kings 1:39 "Zadok the priest took the horn of oil and anointed Solomon ... blew the trumpet. The oil flowed through a sacrificial instrument. The SHOFAR is still used today during the inauguration of each new president in Israel according to Virtualjerusalem.com.

Numbers 29: 1 is interpreted in the Talmud as a command that ALL Jewish males old enough to understand the Torah to hear the sounding of the SHOFAR on Rash Hashanah. If they are unable to attend services, they are to arrange for it to be blown privately for them. The women are not commanded to hear, but it is such a special meeting that they usually voluntarily participate. It is customary that a series of 100 blasts be heard on this day.

"And the seventh month, on the first day of the month, ye shall have a holy convocation; ye shall do no servile work; it is a day of blowing the trumpets unto you." Numbers 29:1

When Rosh Hashanah falls on the Sabbath, the SHOFAR is not sounded in Jewish services for fear that some would violate the law by carrying this horn from one domain to another on the Sabbath rest.

Psalm 47 is to be read just before the blowing of the SHOFAR in this Jewish New Year service. I was excited to learn from a Hebrew scholar that in the original Hebrew, the 1st letter of each of the first verses in this Psalm spell out the words Kera-Satan which means, tear up Satan!!!

The "echo" of the SHOFAR is not considered fulfilling the command, therefore; a recording through electronic equipment would not be considered a legitimate satisfaction of the law.

There are four types of blasts that the Rabbis agreed upon since all the original signals were destroyed when the Temple was destroyed in 70 AD.

T'KIAH is a prolonged blast of any note.
T'RUAH is the shattered note.
SHEVORIM is quavering broken note between two sounds.
TEKIAH GEDOULAH (the Great Tekiah) is the final long extended sound announcing the Messiah is coming to earth.

In ancient times, the SHOFAR blowers would stand on the city wall or mountain tops to announce from city to city the changing of the phases of the moon – and changing of seasons. You might equate it as an official **_audible calendar_**!

Psalm 81:3 "Blow the trumpet in the new moon, in the time appointed..."

Archeologists have discovered a stone in the corner of the Temple Mount in Jerusalem engraved in the ancient language, "For the place of trumpet-blasting."

USING A SHOFAR FOR WARFARE

Used in modem times: For 19 years Syrian troops in the Golan Heights had shelled Israeli Kibbutzim in the valley below. It had been virtually impossible to penetrate their camp up the steep embankments. However, during the Six-Day War in 1967, Shlomo Goren, the chief rabbi of the state flew in a helicopter blowing the SHOFAR while the Israeli stormed the heights. It is recorded that the next day he rode in a tank around the wall of Jerico blowing the SHOFAR and then the following day blew the SHOFAR next to the wall at Jerusalem while Israeli paratroopers entered into and captured the city to make it their capital for the first time in 2,000 years.

In "Days of Awe" it is pointed out that a Greco-Jewish philosopher, Philo, stated the signal on the battlefield to advance and retire was sounded by the SHOFAR, therefore, it is a call of thanks to God who halts war and brings peace and harmony.

Satan, the accuser, wages war on our lives, but God has given us many weapons in which to fight. My mentor, fondly known to our group as Papa Prophet, Rev. Forest Gibbs, did a study on some of the weapons provided. I feel impressed to share a few that include, but are not limited to:

GOD (His many names)	Wisdom
Name of JESUS	Knowledge
HOLY SPIRIT	Understanding
Blood of the Lamb	Vision
WORD of GOD	Prayer
Shield of Faith	Fasting
Truth	Communion
Gifts of the Spirit	Prudence (cautious foreknowledge)
Armor of God (Ephesians 6)	Worship (dance, clap, bow, sing)

Then, of course there are voices, instruments, and tambourines to which there is no use in asking me what is my favorite ***

SHOFARS that are frequently called RAMS HORNS!

WHO BLEW?

"ON EARTH AS IT IS IN HEAVEN"

There are several lines of thought about the SHOFAR blown at Mount Sinai. One says it was Moses who blew the SHOFAR to remind God of HIS covenant with Abraham. Another says it was God's heavenly trumpet and God did the actual blowing. Some people are convinced an Angel blew it because God was talking to Moses and Moses was answering. There is also a theory worth considering that perhaps God's breath (or wind) blowing through the valley and around the mountain may have caused a natural SHOFAR sound. Since it isn't specifically recorded, we don't know, but the most miraculous part is that the SHOFAR was heard above all the thundering, lightening, and quaking.

The first recorded word "trumpet" was in Exodus 19:10-11, 13, *"And the Lord said to Moses: 'Go to the people, and sanctify them today and tomorrow, and let them wash their garments, and be ready against the third day; for the third day, the LORD will come down in the sight of all the people upon mount Sinai, ... when the trumpet sounds long...'"*

This particular Hebrew translation of the SHOFAR suggests this blast was supposedly a continuous sound and only God would be the one who could blast for an indefinite period of time without taking a breath. (For you musicians, there is such a thing as circular breathing, but even then there are slight hesitations in the sound)

The SHOFAR reminds us we will be examined. *AMOS 3:6 "SHALL THE SHOFAR BE BLOWN IN A CITY AND THE PEOPLE NOT TREMBLE? SHALL EVIL BEFALL A CITY AND THE LORD HATH NOT DONE IT?*

Maimones, a Jewish Philosopher said that the SHOFAR calls, "Awake; O you sleepers, awake from your sleep! Search your deeds and turn in repentance. O you who forget the truth in the vanities of time and go astray all the year after vanity and folly that neither profit nor save-remember your Creator! Look at your souls, and better your ways and actions. Let every one of you abandon his evil ways and his wicked thoughts and return to God so that He may have mercy upon you."

BREATHING NEW LIFE

Never despise the times of "VOID" - when you don't seem to be able to see, touch or feel God. To make a point, even God was silent 400 years. It was out of **VOID** that GOD **BEGAN**!!!

Will you allow God to speak a new path into your life? When He does, HE will look and say, "IT IS GOOD."

A curly headed 3 year old walked beside my table at a restaurant. She had a balloon tied to each wrist and was clutching a decorated bag. With a big smile, she pulled out a plastic horn, blew it at me and said, "HAPPY BIRTHDAY TO ME!" My spirit leaped and responded ''yes!'' Had I seen her before? No, but she taught me a great lesson - walk with the expectancy of a little child; celebrate and recognize the changing of seasons! Did she understand the power of anticipation? Probably not. Some people use horns at New Year with a "carnival spirit" to usher in new beginnings; however, the SHOFAR decrees with the HOLY SPIRIT "Happy Birthday" to each new season. In the beginning the Lord hovered and breathed "HAPPY BIRTHDAY WORLD". HE blew into the nostrils of Adam declaring "Happy Birthday Adam". Jehovah-Jirah - the God that supplies our needs-appeared to Abraham through the ram caught by his horns in the thicket, thus "Happy Birthday" to new understanding. HE appeared to the children in the wilderness on the mountaintop introducing a new era and a birth-day present, the Ten Commandments, that will provide loving guidelines for your safety. "Happy Birthday" to the new moon, to the changing of the kings, to the tabernacle – the new location of HIS Spirit to reside. {What do you need "birthed" or "re-birthed"?}

IN ADDITION

- To the enemies in the wilderness - IT'S A NEW SEASON - you WILL receive your just reward!!!

The SHOFAR is even blown at funerals, birthing in the new eternal season of your loved one's life. In Jerusalem, many of the tombstones are inscribed with SHOFARS declaring they are anticipating the last trump to sound when they will arise with the MESSIAH into the heavens.

The very fact God breathed into your nostrils proves HE desires you to be a part of HIS plan!!! HIS breath through you is HIS copyright stamp of approval tattooed upon you until your spirit leaves the confines of your earthly body. HE created and owns the patent and pattern for you!

Could we say here that by changing HIS patent (through following YOUR own plan), you have become a thief?

SYMBOLISM OF THIS "HORN OF PLENTY"

While holding the SHOFAR in my hand, it reminds me of:

THE SERPENT ON THE STICK IN THE WILDERNESS – When the people looked upon it, they were healed.

THE RAM CAUGHT IN THE THICKET by his horns - Rams are highly skilled in going around the thorned bushes and it is highly unusual one would get caught. God provided the blood sacrifice where needed.

THE TWISTED BODY OF CHRIST - He bore our sins on the cross.

A WEAPON - In the hands of Joshua and Gideon's armies.

CONFUSION TO SATAN - Thinking it is the **LAST BLAST** in which the King of kings will take HIS rightful rulership, Satan is totally upset and flees.

"ROD" - God asked Moses, "What's in your hand?" What is in YOUR hand that HE can use?

AN ANIMAL'S POWER AND STRENGTH - The animals butt their heads when fighting for territorial rights. The enemy of your soul wants to fight for ownership. We have dominion over Satan.

ANOINTING VESSEL, HORN OF OIL - Allow the oil of the Holy Spirit to fall upon you and flow through you.

The first time I went to the Oral Roberts Partner Conference, within a mile of campus I felt as if the top of my head was zipped open and warm oil was being poured over me for three days. The shepherd in the field pours oil on the cuts of the sheep not only for healing but to keep the insects from landing and attacking the open wounds.

FIRE ALARM & SMOKE DETECTOR - If the very presence of this instrument should remind Satan that some day the Last Trump should sound, then certainly it should excite you to quickly "check" to see if there's a potential eternal hail, fire and brimstone awaiting you. NOW is the time to clear the smoke and extinguish any sin!

AS A PLOW - To dig up the fallow ground so good seeds can be introduced into the soil of your mind.

BOWING BEFORE HIM - The curves remind us of the position of humbling ourselves, & bowing in HIS presence in prayer and worship.

AMPLIFIER - I like to think of the HOLY SPIRIT as the communications system of God and the SHOFAR as being as a megaphone to get our attention to listen to what HE is saying.

GOD GIVES INSTRUCTIONS, BUT HAVE YOU LISTENED TO HIS FINAL WORDS? LIKE A MYSTERY, SOMETIMES THERE'S A TWIST AT THE END! Shared by Robert Shone CFNI

GOD KNOWS THE ENDING FROM THE BEGINNING *(Isaiah 46:9, 10 "Remember the former things of old: for I AM GOD and there is none else: I AM GOD and there is none like me, Declaring the end from the beginning, and from the ancient times the things that are not yet done, saying, MY counsel shall stand, and I will do all my pleasure."*

ADDITIONAL THOUGHTS

The dinner bell rings and we immediately know it is time to put aside what we are involved in and unite with others to partake of a meal. The SHOFAR blows, and it reminds us that God planned the ultimate banquet for us to enjoy. In Biblical times, the SHOFAR would sound and the people would drop what they were doing and go to observe whatever feast was being celebrated. If two were in the field, two grinding at the mill, two in the bed, the "believer" would leave. Sounds much like a rapture event rehearsal to me!

The factory whistle sounds at the beginning and ending of the day. The SHOFAR reminds us to work while there is still time. The SHOFAR may have been the very FIRST sound to man on earth and may be the very LAST sound on earth man will ever hear!

The cheerleader stands before the spectators to get them involved in proclaiming VICTORY before and during the game. Likewise, the

SHOFAR is an instrument of enthusiasm to encourage the "players" that they have someone to back them.

When the school bell rings we know recess is over and it's time to increase in wisdom and knowledge. The SHOFAR blasts and we realize how much we need to learn. It is time to sit at the feet of Jesus to hear what HE has to say.

The train whistle is used for warning of impending danger if you decide to cross the tracks. I pray you will "hear" the sound of the SHOFAR in your spirit any time you are making a bad decision.

The Emergency Broadcast signal is sounded to inform us of what is happening and to prepare us to seek shelter in the midst of a storm. When you hear the SHOFAR sound, it should encourage you to prepare for the final call when the Messiah comes to take us to His everlasting shelter.

CITING WRITINGS

PHILO, the Greco-Jewish philosopher:
"The SHOFAR was a reminder of the giving of the Torah." (or the first 5 books of the Bible)

Chasidic tradition recalls there was once a SHOFAR blower that was so overwhelmed by the understanding of the service that he couldn't remember what to blow and began weeping. The Rabbi in charge told him not to worry - that his tears were the main message.

ZOHAR, The Jewish Mystics, in the 13th Century:
"Blowing the SHOFAR is like a lover serenading His beloved: Israel seeks to awaken divine love and link the higher and lower worlds."

SAADIAH GAON (882-942 C.E.), Babylonian author:
"When we hear the broken sounds of the SHOFAR, we must also address our prayers to God with hearts broken and full of humility."

RABBI ISAAC:
"If the SHOFAR is NOT sounded at the beginning of the New Year (Rash Hashanah), evil will befall at the end of it. Why so? Because the 'Accuser' [Satan] has not been confused ..."

THE JEWISH MISHNAH (Kinnim 3:6):
When a sacrificial victim dies, its voice is multiplied seven times because:

   1. & 2. its horns become SHOPHARS
   3. & 4. its legs become flutes

5. its hide becomes a drum
6. its entrails are used for lyres
7. its chitterlings for harps

RANDOM THOUGHTS

When blowing the SHOFAR. I do not always have knowledge and understanding of what I am sounding - all I know is that the sounds come from my heart and spirit and I am believing for God to give me the interpretation. There are times when "pictures" flash in my head that give revelation and at other times I don't receive anything to share. Many times when I don't have insight, persons in the audience or congregation will begin weeping, laughing, singing, jumping, or even dancing. This is God's instrument to use as HE chooses. Do you suppose the sequencing of the inspired SHOFAR blowing could be a Morse type code that only the angels, your spirit, or God can interpret accurately?

One of my favorite stories is of a young lad whose father took him for a first time visit to the Jewish Synagogue. Although he didn't understand the service he became so emotional that he began blurting out the Hebrew alphabet. His dad asked him what he was doing and the reply was, "I'm giving God the letters - HE can decide in which order they fit." Have you presented God with whatever gifts, talents or understanding you have? Will you allow HIM to make some final adjustment?

May I encourage you to be responsible to share whatever God given talents you have into the lives of others and leave the results to God.

If you:

play an instrument, you should	-	sow good
sing a song, you should	-	sow good
teach the word, you should	-	sow good

share a smile, you will	-	sow good
whisper a prayer, you will	-	sow good
give unconditional love, you	-	sow good

"SIGN" LANGUAGE REDISCOVERED
OR
SORTING SHOFAR SIGNALS, SIGHTS, SOUNDS & SEASONS

The **SHOFAR OF ASSEMBLY** says,

"Come now up to the mountain of the Lord *** COME, COME. It is now safe to approach me *** Hear what I have to say!!! Exodus 19,20- to which YOU are challenged to respond, "All that the Lord hath spoken, we will do." Exodus 19:8

The **SHOFAR OF WAR** says, "Time to claim what is rightfully yours."

The **SHOFAR OF YESHUA** says, "Look towards the heavenlies". (Yeshua means "salvation") Your redemption draweth nigh.

Our entire life is governed by signals: the light "signals" when it's safe to cross an intersection, an alarm clock "signals" us to wake up, the telephone "signals" us someone wants our attention, an ambulance "signals" there is an emergency. Please allow me the privilege of sharing a few Biblical "SHOFAR SIGNALING SEASONS".

I. ASSEMBLE

Exodus 19:13b " ... *when the trumpet sounded long, they shall come up to the mount"* Numbers 29:1 *"And ye shall have an holy convocation:.. it is a day of blowing the trumpets unto you*

II. CHANGE OF SEASONS & CALL OF FEASTS

Psalm 81:3, 4 *"Blow up the trumpet in the new moon, in the time appointed, on our solemn feast day. For this was a statute for Israel, and a law of the God of Jacob."*

We become a mirror image of whom we spend the most time. Is it HIM?

III. CONSECRATE YOURSELF AND FAST

Joel 2:15, 16, 17 *"Blow the trumpet in Zion, sanctify a fast, call a solemn assembly... sanctify the congregation ... let the bridegroom go forth of His chamber, and the bride out of her closet. Let the priests, the ministers of the Lord, weep between the porch and the altar, and let them say, Spare thy people, O Lord ..."*

IV. RECOGNIZE HIS PRESENCE

Joshua 6:8 *" ... seven priests bearing the seven trumpets of rams' horns passed on before the Lord, and blew with the trumpets: and the ark of the covenant of the Lord followed them."*

II Samuel 6:15 *"So David and all the house of Israel brought up the ark of the Lord with shouting, and with the sound of the trumpet."*

1 Chronicles 16:6 RSV *"Beniah and Yahaziel the priests were to blow the trumpets continually before the ARK"*

We are sometimes so busy doing FOR HIM that we fail to recognize we are to spend time WITH HIM.

V. REPENT AND CHANGE

Isaiah 58:1 *"Cry aloud, spare not, lift up thy voice like a trumpet, and shew my people their transgression ..."*

Jeremiah 6:17 *"Also I set watchmen over you, saying, Hearken to the sound of the trumpet. But they said, "We will not hearken."*

The SHOFAR can be considered as a representation of a prophet's voice.

VI. SEAL AN OATH

II Chronicles 15:12,14 *"And they entered into a covenant to seek the Lord God of their fathers with all their heart and with all their soul ... they sware unto the Lord with a loud voice, and with shouting, and with trumpets and with cornets."*

VII. TRANSPORT THE ARK OF THE COVENANT

I Chronicles 15:28 *"Thus all Israel brought up the ark of the covenant of the LORD with shouting, and with sound of the cornet* (ram's horn), *and with trumpets ..."*

VIII. SOLOMAN DEDICATED THE TEMPLE

II Chronicles 5:1,12-14 *"Thus all the work that Solomon made for the house of the Lord was finished ... with them an hundred and twenty priests sounding with trumpets ... the trumpeters and singers were as one, to make one sound heard in praising and thanking the Lord ... when they lifted up their voice with the trumpets and cymbals and instruments of music ... the house was filled with a cloud ... so that the priests could not stand to minister;.. for the glory of the Lord had filled the house of God"*

IX. FOUNDATION OF THE SECOND TEMPLE

Ezra 3:10 *"when the builders laid the foundation of the temple of the Lord, they set the priests in their apparel with trumpets ..."*

X. DEDICATE THE WALL AT JERUSALEM

Nehemiah 12:27, 35 *"And at the dedication of the wall of Jerusalem they sought the Levites out of all their places ... and certain of the priests' sons with trumpets..."*

XI. PROCLAIM LIBERTY * ATONEMENT

Leviticus 25:9, 10 *"Then shalt thou cause the trumpet of the jubilee to sound on the tenth day of the seventh month, in the day of atonement shall ye make the trumpet sound throughout all your land"*

XII. WARN OF APPROACHING DANGER

Ezekiel 33:3-6 *"If he seeth the sword come upon the land, he blow the trumpet, and warn the people: Then whosoever heareth the sound of the trumpet, and taketh not warning.... his blood shall be upon his own head.... he that taketh warning shall delivereth his soul. But if the watchman see the sword come, and blow not the trumpet, and the people be not warned: if the sword come, and take any person from among them, he is taken away in his iniquity: but his blood will I require at the watchman's hand"*

XIII. CALL TO WAGE WAR

Jeremiah 4:19,21 *"My bowels, my bowels! I am pained at my very heart: my heart maketh a noise in me: I cannot hold my peace, because thou has heard, O my soul, the sound of the trumpet, the alarm of war ... How long shall I see the standard, and hear the sound of the trumpet?"*

I Corinthians 14:8,9 *"For if the trumpet give an uncertain sound, who shall prepare himself to the battle?"*

XIV. ALLOW GOD TO FIGHT FOR US

Numbers 10:9 *" ... if you go to war ... against enemy that oppresseth you, then ye shall blow an alarm with the trumpets; and ye shall be* remembered before the Lord your God .. ye shall be saved from your enemies.

What enemy is oppressing you? God will fight the battle. As a word of reminder, be willing to fight along side HIM!!!

XV. BREAK DOWN WALLS * CONQUER THE ENEMY

Joshua 6:20 *"So the people shouted when the priests blew with the trumpets ... the people heard the sound of the trumpet ... the wall fell down flat ... they took the city."*

XVI. CONFUSION TO THE ENEMY

Judges 7:16-22 *" ...and he [Gideon] put a trumpet in every man's hand ... and the three hundred blew the trumpets, and the Lord set every man's sword against His fellow, even throughout all the host: and the host fled..."*

XVII. SACRIFICIAL SUBSTITUTION

Genesis 22:13,14 *"... Abraham lifted up His eyes, and looked, and behold behind him a ram caught in a thicket by his horns, and Abraham went and took the ram, and offered him up for a burnt offering in the stead of his son. "* Have YOU lifted up your eyes, looked, and taken hold of the offering GOD HAS PROVIDED?

XVIII. WORSHIP

Isaiah 27:13 *"... the great trumpet shall be blown, and they shall come.., and shall worship the Lord in the holy mount at Jerusalem. "* .

Psa1m 98:6 *"With trumpets and sound of cornet make a joyful noise before the Lord, the King."*

Psalm 150:3 *"Praise him with the sound of the trumpet."*

Revelation 11:15 *"and the seventh angel sounded [blew trumpet]: and there were great voices in heaven, saying, . "The kingdoms of this world are become the kingdoms of our Lord, and of His Christ [Messiah]: and He shall reign forever and ever."*

XIX. CORONATION OF KINGS

I Kings 1:39 *"And Zadok the priest took an horn of oil out of the tabernacle, and anointed Solomon. And they blew the trumpet: and all the people said, God save King Solomon."*

II Kings 11:12-14 *" ... put the crown upon him ... behold the king stood by a pillar, as the manner was, and the princes and trumpeters by the king, and all the people of the land rejoiced, and blew with trumpets ..."*

It didn't matter if the kings did good or evil in the sight of the Lord - they were still honored because of the office.

XX. YESHUA IS COMING BACK

I Corinthians 15:52 *"In a moment, in the twinkling of an eye, at the last trump: for the trumpet shall sound, and the dead shall be raised incorruptible, and we shall be changed"*

I Thessalonians 4:16 *"For the Lord himself shall descend from heaven with a shout, with the voice of the archangel, and with the trump of God..."*

XXI. JUDGEMENT DAYS

Revelation 8-10 *" ... there was silence in heaven about the space of half an hour. And I saw the seven angels, which stood before God: and to them were given seven trumpets... the seven angels which had the seven trumpets prepared themselves to sound The first angel sounded, and there followed hail and fire mingled with blood, and they were cast upon the earth: second angel sounded... a great mountain burning with fire was cast into the sea...third angel sounded and there fell a great star from heaven, burning as it were a lamp... forth angel sounded, and the third part of the sun was smitten... I beheld, and heard an angel flying through the midst of heaven, saying with a loud voice, "Woe, woe, woe, to the inhibiters of the earth by reason of the other voices of the trumpet of the three angels, which are yet to sound ... And the fifth angel sounded, and I saw a star fall from heaven unto the earth: and to him was given the key of the bottomless pit. And he opened the bottomless pit; and there arose a smoke ... out of the smoke locusts ... given power, as the scorpions of the earth have power. .. and it was commanded them that they should not hurt... only those men which have not the seal of God in their foreheads ... they should not kill them, but that they should be tormented five months and their torment was as torment of a scorpion, when he striketh a man ... in those days shall men seek death, and shall not find it; and shall desire to die, and death shall flee from them ... the sixth angel sounded, and I heard a voice from the four horns of the golden altar which is before God, Saying to the sixth angel which had the trumpet, Loose the four angels which are bound in the great river Euphrates. And the four angels were loosed, which were prepared for an hour, and a day, and a month, and a year, for to slay the third part of men... but in the days of the voice of the seventh angel, when he shall begin to sound [trumpet] the mystery of God should be finished as he hath declared to His servants the prophets."*

REVELATION 1:3 "BLESSED IS HE THAT READETH, AND THEY THAT HEAR THE WORDS OF THIS PROPHECY, AND KEEP THOSE THINGS WHICH ARE WRITTEN THERIN; FOR THE TIME IS AT HAND."

I do not pretend to be able to interpret those scriptures about the seven angels, but I do intend to keep reading THE WORD and be blessed!!!

ANYTHING WE BECOME REQUIRES A PROCESS

The SHOFAR is cut, boiled, softened, gutted, put under pressure, put through the fire, twisted and bent, punctured and bore out, sanded, polished, inspected, and then USED. How many times have you said,

"Use me Lord" without thinking of the process it will take before you are ready for him to blow through you? And just remember, the SHOFAR that doesn't yield goes back into the boiling pot or cast aside. Many are called, but few are chosen. Matthew 20:16 *"So the last shall be first, and the first last: for many be called, but few chosen."* You may not know what part of the process your brother or sister is going through themselves, so give them a little slack – they might be in a whole LOT OF HURT.

SAVOR THE SEASONS

There is a corporate season where the body, group, or church moves forward much as the Israelites moved from the wilderness to the Promised Land. Within that group each individual was going through their own seasons. Some had just lost their loved ones, some were anxious to get to the other side, some were apprehensive of leaving what was familiar, (no matter how bad it was, there was still comfort in knowing what to expect) and some were fearful of what they would become if they had everything. They preferred to remain status quo because they didn't trust themselves. I am reminded that in the spring season while plants are developing, God's plan is they don't come forth at the same rate. Think of a beautiful year round garden where the spectators have something fresh to gaze upon no matter the season. Since we do not enter the same seasons at the same time, let us have respect for the season another person is going through.

What "season" are YOU experiencing? Slowly consider* would it be:

simplicity, satisfaction, surprise, shaking, sifting, surrendering, sobbing, salvation, sanctifying, sharing, sedating, sacrificing, simmering, surgery; stitching, submission, sealing, shouting, silence, saturation, sameness, and the final result of passing through these passage ways is

SHALOM (peace)

CONCLUSION

"I'M COMING BACK"

I Thes. 4.'16 For the Lord himself shall descend from heaven with a shout, with the voice of the archangel, and with the trump of God.

It was a spectacular sunset that summer at Camp Vespers at Mt. Wesley in Kerrville, TX. I was about 15 years old, and knew very little scripture. Suddenly there projected forth a figure from the clouds. It was a brilliant outline of a person in a flowing robe – the face was pure light with no features and it stopped approximately a third of the way from the clouds to where I was sitting on: those old concrete steps. Then I heard a voice gently say, "I'm coming back." Then it melted back into the clouds and I sat frozen in my seat for maybe a half hour. In my mind I said "Jesus just spoke to me – how could that be possible?" It was such an intimate visit that it was almost ten years later that I could even tell someone - and that was after I read the scriptures relating to Jesus' return. I remember moving my eyes around to see if anyone else was responding, but it seemed that everyone was listening to the preacher.

Was I so special that HE chose to reveal Himself to me? No, I believe that it was HIS way of preparing my heart to share HIS truth with others. One of my greatest downfalls (but also a strength because I am skeptical of everyone else's winds of doctrine until I'm confident it is truth) is unbelief.

This phenomenon impacted my life. I challenge you to request God to reveal HIMSELF to you personally in His own unique way. Once you have experienced a supernatural visitation or have heard His voice, I can guarantee it will remove all doubt of His reality.

There are two things to remember:

A. We have not because we ask not

B. Blessed are they who do not see and yet believe (this will remind you not to be too proud that He showed up!)

The SHOFAR is known as perhaps the only instrument that demands a response. When it sounds, it announces the presence of the King:

> some will bow
> some will worship
> some will stand at attention/march/dance/rejoice/shout/ sing/play instruments
> some will be at ease
> some will try to flee,
> but all, I said all, will respond.

While in Washington D.C, I instinctively curtseyed in front of a foreign leader. When we hear that FINAL EARTH SHAKING EVENT in the day that the GREAT SHOFAR SOUNDS, announcing the FINAL CORONATION of THE ETERNAL KING, "every knee will bow before Him and every tongue will proclaim that He is Lord"

Romans 14: 10,11 ... for we shall all stand before the judgment seat of Christ. For it is written ... every knee shall bow ... and every tongue shall confess ... then every one of us shall give account of himself to God

Why wait until you think He's coming back to honor, praise, and worship HIM.

It is the author's opinion that the SHOFAR is a musical chord that is woven into the pages of the Bible, from beginning to end, that opens us to the very awareness that our King of kings, and Lord of lords, the Master Judge and Ruler of the Universe desires for each of us to reign with HIM eternally. We. are each a part of HIS heavenly orchestra - what a shame it would be for your seat to remain empty after the last trump shall sound. Won't you take a moment right now to ask, whether for the first time, or renew your vow, Yeshua, Jesus Christ into your life? II Corinthians 13:5 says, *"Examine yourselves, whether ye be in the faith; prove your own selves..."*

An old Rabbi saying is "God always creates the antidote BEFORE the sickness." Before the foundation of the earth, God planned forgiveness and salvation through Jesus of Nazareth.

When you say "I'll repent later" you are really guilty of premeditated rebellion. You can become oblivious to God's wooing. Solomon says the best time to repent is in your youth. Procrastination is actually disobedience in slow motion.

Someone said, "God doesn't find out about our sin when we confess it, but that is when HE instantly forgets it". CONFESS ONCE AND QUIT REMINDING HIM. Remember that God chides and reproves, but it is Satan who condemns.

Won't you stop reading for a moment, raise your arms in surrender, and ask HIM to become Lord over your life. May His peace and unspeakable joy flood you and your domain today and forever more.

May the reading of these words I have written bring faith, hope, comfort, promise, instruction, information, and most of all a new or renewed determination to seek and serve our Lord and Savior.

Lord. I lift my friend up to You, right now in the mighty name of YESHUA, Jesus of Nazareth. And ask that You anoint them with the oil of peace, gladness and joy. May they. have Your supernatural

33

Janet Rae Askins

wisdom and, knowledge about the season they are experiencing while reading this book. I ask, Loving Father, that You give each one the Holy Spirit to administer Your unconditional love, and challenge You to become so very real and personal in their life. I love You, Lord, and are expectant about Your coming. Amen

P.S. I asked the Lord what HE had to say to His people, that's you, for this hour. He showed me a picture of a ram with his head down and horns bursting through a wall and said, "People think they are up against a brick wall, but it's only an image of bricks painted on the paper. If they will press in with the power, authority, and anointing I've given them, they will tear through.

BREAK THROUGH THAT MIRAGE AND EXPERIENCE WHAT GOD HAS FOR YOU!!! Hold fast to the horns of the altar and ALTER YOUR LIFE TODAY - ENJOY THE RIDE. {You'll never be bored again!}

SHALOM, SHALOM SELAH

Because of HIS LOVE for you,
A Fresh Beginning...

THE SHOFARIST SYNOPSIS

I WILL ENDEAVOR TO:

- Be-have Thyself: conduct yourself wisely at all times.
- Be full of integrity
- Be gracious when the shofar playing is rejected...because it will happen.
- Be a good representative of all Shofarists. My conduct will influence how others view Shofarists.
- Be a workman who has studied and shown myself approved.
- Be full of Love, Joy, Peace, Patience, Kindness, Goodness, Faithfulness, Gentleness and Self-control!
- Be in submission to the person in authority at all events; Honor and follow their instructions.
- Be under the authority / submission / leadership of an anointed pastor or apostle.
- Be respectful and sensitive to other Shofarists.
- Be willing to teach others the techniques and protocols I have learned.

Be continually sensitive to the leading of the Holy Spirit.

Section 2

SHOFAR NOTES

FOREWORD

It is an honor to write the forward for a true Shofar psalmist. I have known Janet Rae Askins for over a decade and have been privileged to labor alongside her in a variety of settings for the kingdom of God. She is an anointed vessel of the Lord for this hour. I have heard her release the sound of heaven into the earth in a number of kingdom gatherings. Each time, you knew that the Father was calling us to attention in order to hear vital instructions for this hour. As we listened, we were never disappointed. The teaching you hold in your hand is a necessary part of equipping the Body of Christ for spiritual warfare. Because many people do not know (or could be better instructed) in the prophetic significance of the sound(s) of the Shofar they miss an opportunity for "open heavens" in their life. Read prayerfully the revelation God has given Janet and be enlightened. Be open to respond to the sound of the Shofar and be blessed.

Dr. Walter Fletcher
Desert Rivers International
Dallas, Texas
April 2008

INTRODUCTION

While ministering at a church in the early days of my Shofar demonstrations, I, Janet Rae, made the comment to the congregation, "If anyone knows a good mentor on the Shofar, will you please introduce me to them?" Much to my surprise I was immediately reprimanded by the Holy Ghost saying, "You already have the best mentor – ME." Oh how I had to ask for instant forgiveness. Yes, He will teach us all things when we diligently seek His face. From that day forward, I've sought HIS direction and wisdom of how this instrument should be used and shared. It is my privilege to document what I have learned, but encourage you to seek the Lord's further instructions to you personally. He may have additional things for you to accomplish and promote. We all have our own measure of understanding, gifts, and experiences that will influence our particular ministry and please use this booklet as only a guideline for what the Lord wants YOU to accomplish.

Whether there are 10 or 1,000 people hearing the sounds, it seems God personalizes a unique message for each person. In the future, we will be documenting the testimonies of how lives were touched and changed by these heavenly love notes.

Why call this portion of the booklet Shofar Notes? The English language has many descriptions of "note" that reminds me of the many functions of the Shofar.

1. Note - a short informal letter - the Lord communicates to us through the various sounds of the Shofar.
2. Note - a certain quality, hint, or trace - the Shofar stirs up emotions we may ordinarily fail to recognize.

3. Note - formal letter from one government to another the Shofar brings messages from the heavens and earth together - it requires a response.
4. Note - to make a record or memorandum of - the Shofar experience will be written on the tablets of your heart.
5. Music Note - tone made by an instrument or voice - the Voice within the voice of the Shofar can represent the Voice of God.
6. Note - legal paper acknowledging a debt and promising to pay - the Shofar reminds us of God's covenant by sending Jesus to pay our debts and usher us to heaven some day.
7. Note - attention, heed, notice - the Shofar is used to awaken our senses.
8. Note - take notes to exchange ideas, suggestions, and facts to remember - I pray that the wisdom learned from my experiences will help you accomplish your vision.

Each "note" of the Shofar seems to carry it's own message, instruction, or whatever pleases the Lord to portray to each individual. It is stimulating to study this Biblical instrument as God continues to unfold it's mystery.

MAY YOU ENJOY LEARNING MORE ABOUT GOD'S
ANOINTED INSTRUMENT THROUGH

SHOFAR NOTES

SIGNALING THE SEASONS

(The Biblical Significance of the Shofar/Ram's Horn)

The TRUMPET OF THE LORD says, **"Come now up to the mountain of the Lord *****COME, COME. It is now safe to approach me *** Hear what I have to say!!!"** ***** **Exodus 19, 20** To which YOU are challenged to respond, **"All that the Lord hath spoken, we will do."** **Exodus 19:8**

The **SHOFAR** signals, "CHANGE" *** Ecclesiastes 3:1-8 It reminds us to pay attention to the **TIMING OF THE LORD:**

I	ASSEMBLE	Exodus 19:13b
II	CONSECRATION & FASTING	Joel 2:15.16
III	RECOGNIZE HIS PRESENCE	I Chronicles 16:6
IV	REPENT	Isaiah 58:1
V	PROCLAIM LIBERTY *Jubilee	Leviticus 25:9,10
VI	ALLOW GOD TO FIGHT FOR US	Numbers 10:9
	(& we are willing to fight alongside)	
VII	CONFUSION TO THE ENEMY	Judges 7:16-21
	(SHOFAR used as weapon)	
VIII	BREAKING DOWN WALLS	Joshua 6:20
IX	OFFERINGS	Numbers 10:10
X	SACRIFICE SUBSTITUTION	Genesis 22:13,14
XI	YESHUA IS COMING BACK	I Thessalonians 4:16

Have YOU: recognized and are repentant of your sins, asked Yeshua (Jesus) to become Lord and Savior of your life, renounced the workings of Satan in your life, asked HIM to reveal Himself to you through the

Holy Spirit, and agreed to obey whatever HE commands you to do? If not, why not do it NOW!

***NOW IS THE DAY OF SALVATION ***

"Call upon HIM while HE can be found and HE will show you great & mighty things, which thou knowest not." Jeremiah 33:3

SHOFAR – NOTES

Taught by Janet Rae Askins – SHOFAR PSALMIST

Welcome to explore with me the fundamentals of bringing glory to God through the use of the Biblical trumpet known as the Ram's Horn or Jubal Horn which we will refer to as the Hebrew word "SHOFAR".

It's been my custom to examine new challenges and information; therefore I welcome any comments, suggestions and constructive criticism. As we share in experiencing new ideas, the overall plan of God will be implemented.

Shall we begin?

As you take this journey, you might INCREASE understanding of:

Exodus 19:5
Now therefore, if ye will obey my voice indeed, and keep my covenant, then ye shall be a **peculiar** treasure unto me above all people: for all the earth is mine:

1 Corinthians 1:27
But God hath chosen the **foolish** things of the world to **confound** the wise; and God hath chosen the weak things of the world to **confound** the things which are mighty;

2 Timothy 2:15
Study to shew thyself **approved** unto God, a workman that needeth not to be ashamed, rightly dividing the word of truth.

AND MOST IMPORTANT THOUGHT:

GLORY, GLORY, GLORY
HOLY, HOLY, HOLY ART THOU
OH GOD - CREATER OF THE UNIVERSE
WHO TEACHES US ALL THINGS!!!

WORDS OF ADVICE

BE SEEN - BUT NOT NECESSARILY HEARD

As a sanctified note-tooter you will want to present yourself in a professional manner.

Here are a few suggestions of protocol that the Lord has shown me. You will need to constantly refer to HIS instruction for every conceivable season of service – and as HIS ambassador, you will want to be adaptable in order to be invited back!

WHEN YOU FIRST GET YOUR SHOFAR, note that not everyone will have an appreciation for your carrying an "animal horn" into the service.
You can expect odd looks and snide remarks. Keep your heart sweet and tender towards their uneducated comments. Many times a smile and silence is your best defense.

BE AWARE OF WHERE YOUR SHOFAR IS AT ALL TIMES.
Swinging it into someone's body or face is unacceptable behavior! Be careful not to knock something over or place your horn on the floor where someone can trip.

YOU WILL AUTOMATICALLY CREATE A DISTURBANCE WHEN BRINGING A SHOFAR INTO THE BUILDING.
Try not to call attention to it. I can guarantee people will see it - it seems to carry its own anointing.

THE FIRST TIME YOU GO TO AN ASSEMBLY, ASK TO SEE THE HEAD USHER OR PERSON RESPONSIBLE FOR THE SERVICE.
Explain to them who you are, and reassure them you are not here to interrupt the service, but are available to be a blessing if they should ask you to play.

IF THEY ARE FAMILIAR WITH THE SHOFAR, ASK IF IT IS OK IF YOU PLAY DURING THE PRAISE SERVICE WHEN IT FITS IN WITH THE MUSIC.
In the event they say "NO" – then honor their wishes. If they say they prefer you not to play, or they don't know, then don't.

IT IS APPROPRIATE TO MAKE AN APPOINTMENT TO VISIT A PASTOR, BUSINESS OWNER OR HEAD OF ORGANIZATION A WEEK IN ADVANCE – ESPECIALLY IF YOU SENSE STRONGLY THAT YOU SHOULD BLOW IN THEIR CHURCH OR AREA OF THEIR DOMAIN.
Explain why you would like to bless them, your exact intentions and ask if they would like to fit you in. This would be an excellent time to request or make plain any financial arrangements. It is always best to have a member of the church/organization to open this door for you and endorse your reputation.

SPEAK WITH AUTHORITY WHILE BEING GRACIOUS
Not everyone will appreciate the SHOFAR ministry. Don't apologize for your anointing, but remember that the Lord exalts the humble and your gift WILL make room for you…(perhaps in another location!)

DRESS APPROPRIATELY
Remember whom you are representing! Anyone planning to minister should normally be dressed better than 50% of the audience. Clothing does make a difference of how you are received. If you only have one nice outfit, wear it with dignity – and make sure it is clean and pressed.

SMELL GOOD --- This goes for you AND your SHOFAR!
A breath mint, deodorant, and cologne for yourself makes you much more tolerable! We'll cover keeping your SHOFAR clean in another section.

SO YOU WANT TO BE A SHOFAR SOWER?

A checkpoint chapter for **anyone** in ministry

To go to the next level in school you must take a test to determine if you qualify. While our spirit is open, let us ask these vital questions. Based on the answers, would you honestly promote yourself to the next level if YOU were the teacher?

Ultimately, **GOD** hands out the grades: therefore man's grades aren't quite as important!

SOMETIMES GOD'S TESTS ARE FILL IN THE BLANKS, MULTIPLE CHOICE, OR ESSAY QUESTIONS WHERE THERE IS NOT JUST ONE ANSWER.
Question your servant hood!!!

1. Am I drawing attention to myself, my God given talent   OR   Attention to HIM?

2. Am I trying to impress my family or friends   OR   Please FATHER?

3. Is it just fun   OR   Does it minister? Isaiah 62:1-3

4. There's no one else around to do this   OR   I'M APPOINTED? (by the Holy Spirit)

5. It's a skill not too   OR   I'M ANOINTED?
    many can do

6. I'll make myself known   OR   I'll give GLORY to GOD?

7. I'll hoard this gift   OR   I'll not only share it but I'll help
                                    others succeed: especially if it's
                                    the same type gifting

PURPOSE IN YOUR HEART TO LET THE GIFTS LEAD THE WAY TO THE THRONE -- INSTEAD OF BLOCKING THE WAY TO THE THRONE. (UNKNOWN)

If you are denied the privilege to minister, are you upset, critical, jealous, or hurt? Experience has taught me that God watches our reactions and if we pass this test, there is an even greater opportunity to bring glory to HIS name later: therefore, repent if necessary and take the test over!!! Here's a word of caution though:

DON'T BE SO DETERMINED TO DO EVERYTHING SO PERFECT THAT YOU DO NOTHING!!

Several times I have been guilty of being "performance" oriented. Where we are weak, HE is strong, and I like to remember that where we are strong, HE is weak!

Be a **FUNatic** ** If you do not enjoy serving in a particular category, then seek HIS counsel and determine if you have set yourself in the position, have been pushed into it by well meaning people, or is this a time of stretching your limits by the Lord for this season. (Given by the Holy Spirit to Janet Rae 11-22-96 in class at Christ for The Nations. I encourage you to enjoy serving Him – He has such a sense of humor – after all, He made us!!!)

Many SHOFAR blowers have created costumes to wear when they go into churches, conventions, or various situations. You may desire to do some biblical research on the Priestly robes and their functions and design your own. I have a beautiful Priest ephod that fits over several outfits and a variety of Tallit – or the Jewish Prayer Shawls to wear. Men generally wear white tunics with golden sashes over white shirts and pants or Biblical garments. You are not limited except by your imagination but please ask the person in charge what is appropriate before you show up or give a program. You may prefer to wear your Sabbath best.

SPECIFICALLY FOR THE NOTE – TOTE - TOOTER

You may be asking, "OK, so exactly what notes are appropriate?" Shall we refer to the Jewish customs?

The original patterns were lost during the burning of the Temple in 70 AD and a group of Rabbis made some guidelines of specific "calls" to sound many years later. They have incorporated several different usages of the following notes.

The specific SHOFAR calls are: **(I'm using the "O" as one note and the "E" as a higher note – This method is the JANET RAE VERSION as a means of interpretation)**

TEKIAH - universally accepted as a clear sounding long blast.

TOOOOOOOOOOOOOOOOOOOOOOOOOOOOOOOEEE

This is also spelled t'kiah and is equated to an alarm to awaken your senses.

SHEVARIM - a broken sigh of three shorter cries.

TOOOOOOEEE - TOOOOOOEEE - TOOOOOOEEE

48

Another spelling is sh'varim also resembles as wailing.

TERUAH - the staccato or quick pumping
series of 9 or more short notes.

TOTOTOTOTOTOTOTOTOTOTOOO
- TOTOTOTOTOTOTOTOTOTOTOOO
- TOTOTOTOTOTOTOTOTOTOTOOO

The optional spelling is t'ruah and it reminds us of broken promises and vows we have made.

And the FINAL CALL

TEKIAH GEDOLAH - an unbroken blast that you hold out as long as you can - it is called THE GREAT TEKIAH AS BLOWN BY GOD

TOOOOOOOOOOOOOOOOOOOOOOOOOOOOOOOOOOOOOOOOOOOOO
OOOOOOOOOOOOOOOOOOEEEEEEEEEEEE

Where Can I Play?

The following list is not limited – it is only a guideline and suggestion:

It is wise to prepare a printed short paragraph explaining the SHOFAR and what it represents for the person introducing you. Most people do not have any knowledge of why you are blowing or what the SHOFAR is all about. You can also introduce it yourself, but I personally like to save my wind and be praying before I blow.

Call to assembly - at any function that has a foundation lifting the name of Jehovah. It could be at conventions, business dedications, civic organizations, stockholder's meetings, churches, anniversaries, and intercessor's meetings. I normally use the more traditional Tekiah, Shevarim, Teruah, and Tekiah Gedolah for these type meetings to begin instead of ad lib.

Sealing an oath or sealing a prophecy – As the spirit leads.

Playing and praying over the sick – I often get impressions to blow in the area of where they need healing – the feet, back, arms, etc. You do not have to always blow facing them.

Warfare – Use the militant sounds with staccato notes.

Pronouncing a Blessing over someone – you might receive some words you would like to share to edify that person while blowing.

Weddings – Often the very first function and normally relating the blowing of the SHOFAR to Jesus calling His Bride. These are usually lively sounds.

Funerals – The minister in charge will know specifically when he wants you to play. I usually blow long notes as the Spirit leads and a little softer than normal. Then I sometimes play "TAPS" over the casket either at the end or while they are lowering the body.

Home dedications – A short service setting apart your new home for God's glory or rededication of your home.

Redeeming the Land – Going to the four corners of the land and dedicating it to the Lord. Several SHOFAR blowers I know go to Indian Reservations and ask for peace among the nations. I go to courthouses and blow that there will be righteous government – beware you do not blow without permission in public places from someone in authority unless it might be outside in the open. If you are asked to quit, pack up and leave without confrontation.

SOUNDS

At a facility where I was once working we were allowed to wear headphones and I was listening to some Praise Music. The gentleman who shared the cubicle asked politely, "Is that you tapping on the desk?" Suddenly I realized that each of us were in the same office, but hearing something quite different. Could each of us be in the same church, community, and even our homes and hear our faithful Father give us a different set of instructions? How dare we dispute what another "hears" unless it does not line up with the WORD of GOD. Often we take our love notes from heaven and try to persuade others it is the ONLY letter HE has written and we have all the answers!!!

Often I blow two SHOFARS at the same time. They came from two different animals and were purchased six months apart through different vendors. Though they are similar, they are quite unique. Since you can actually trim the horns to produce a certain note, I "told" the Lord that the new one was slightly out of tune & I would trim it to exactly match the first one I'd purchased. He rebuked me and said, "Don't change a thing! That is their unique sound and leave it that way." How many times have you tried to "help God out"? How many times are we guilty of trying to be something we are not? We either try to improve on God's plan for ourselves or we try to change someone else to fit into what we think they should be.

The animals have a knowing their horns were made for their own use - to display their power and to use for battle. Are we sometimes mimicking the animals, thinking our gifts are to be used for our own benefit? The horns were grown and prepared, but it wasn't until the animal was sacrificed that these horns could be used for God's purposes. How much sacrifice are you willing to go through to be used for the kingdom?

When the SHOFAR is embellished with silver, gold, or wrappings, it normally will not vibrate as well and sound will be hindered. Are you so "embellished" with nonsense that people can't clearly "hear" what you say? Forget all the "fluff" and serve the God Stuff!!!

ONE ANOINTED NOTE IS BETTER THAN AN ENTIRE SKILLFULLY PLAYED CARNAL CANTATA.

He Speaks
He Prepares
He's Purchased Us
He Places Us - if we'll obey

You must be in the right place. These SHOFARS have a distinct sound in various places and perform different functions with the same techniques and amount of effort.

The signals I played at a meeting of about 1,200 intercessors who flew in from all over the world was used to excite the crowd one evening and the next morning, to my surprise, the exact same signals were used to calm them. What's the difference? It was the anointing HE wanted us to experience!!!

He Authorizes Us
He Anoints Us
He Appoints Us

SACRIFICIAL SOUND

Derek and DeDe Kuhn had a Rosh Hashanah service in 1997 where I was formally introduced to the Biblical SHOFAR and blessed to sit under Derek's teaching. You can imagine how spine tingling it was to hear approximately 25 SHOFARS blasting at the same time by both children and adults.

Derek stated, "The blast is a sound that reminds Satan of that blood sacrifice that was provided by God Himself when Abraham offered Isaac on the altar. We know that Isaac was a type of Jesus and His giving of His life for us; therefore, the sound reminds Satan of the cross. The ram caught in the thicket by the horns was the substitute offering and His horns were the symbol of the authority and strength of the animal. The ram has excellent maneuvering abilities and it was highly unlikely for one to be caught in the brush - - Are you willing to be "caught" to be used for God's purposes??

It was from Derek and DeDe that I purchased my first and favorite SHOFAR during a Worship Conference at Christ For The Nations in November 1997.

GOD GRAVITATOR

USHERING THE PEOPLE INTO THE PRESENCE OF GOD is in my opinion is the most significant function of our SHOFAR.

When blowing the sounds, I sometimes visualize our trying to get the attention of God. A certain King in Africa said that when he is arriving into a village and hears the drums and/or music in the background, his spirit is stirred and he is ready to receive and more open to grant the people's request. When my children Carolin Renee and Marilyn Janae were tiny and wanted my attention, they would grab me around the leg or pull on my skirt and though at times it seemed inconvenient to stop and listen, it always warmed my heart they came to me in trust and love. Likewise, we tug on the hem of HIS garment through various means. The SHOFAR reminds God of HIS covenants with us.

Know when to be silent! Remember Jesus before the Sanhedrin. Don't waste energy on someone who won't/can't receive from the ministry God has entrusted to you.

Be a peacemaker or a pacesetter, but not a performer and prover. You don't have to boast of your value - those in need or those who are able to discern will discern the significance of your blasts!

A STRONG WORD OF CAUTION

Always plead the Blood of Jesus over yourself (silently of course) when you end an event. You have invaded the enemy territory and it is not unusual to experience some retaliating spirits being manifest in unusual ways. Be careful driving home, watch your step, and put a guard on your emotions. This explanation is not to scare you – it is to prepare you.

DON'T GET IN A RUT, PLAY FROM YOUR GUT!

OK, this sounds a little graphic, but be sensitive to the Holy Spirit's lead in the service. God may want to use your blowing as a transition. Even if you think you know what He has given you to play, be flexible. I was once half way through a peaceful blow & suddenly went into a warfare type signal. It totally changed the atmosphere - I asked the drums to join me, only to find out later that a young man in the service had just made a decision that required him to give up some music he had been listening to. We, the drums & SHOFAR, gave this young man a new beat to carry in his heart. He may have been the only person who needed that sound, but remember the shepherd that left the 99 to find that one that was lost. The Holy Spirit will go totally out of HIS way to change the service to fulfill HIS promise to that praying Grandma or intercessor.

I ONCE HEARD ED COLE SAY:
"HEAR FROM GOD AND IMPART TO PEOPLE - DON'T
SPEAK TO PEOPLE AND THEN TELL GOD TO BLESS IT!
YOU MUST HAVE THE RHEMA WORD"
I WOULD LIKE TO ADD:
YOU SHOULD HAVE A RHEMA SHOFAR PATTERN TO PLAY!

It was interesting to look up the word "embouchure" in Webster's Dictionary. You musicians will think of this word as the mouth hole on an instrument or the placement of the lips on a mouthpiece. These definitions are correct, but the very first example in the dictionary is "a mouth of a river". Doesn't the Word say, "Rivers of living water will flow from your belly"?

JOHN 7:38

Hosea 14:2 reads "...Take away all iniquity, and receive us graciously: so will we render the calves of our lips." The calves or fruit of our lips means the praise of our lips will be offered in place of the sacrifice of animals.

As you blow the SHOFAR be reminded you are releasing the Holy Spirit within you and through your breath and lips:

LET THE RIVERS FLOW.

INVOLVING OTHERS ON THE PLATFORM

IF YOU HAVE THE NEED TO OUT-DO SOMEONE, OUT-LOVE THEM!!!

If you have confidence in the praise & worship musicians and they are flowing in the gifts, don't hesitate to ask them individually to join you at some point in your playing - especially if you are calling out and blessing individuals. (Please do not call people out unless you are specifically instructed by the Holy Spirit - this is not a ministry to see who you can impress – it is a ministry to see who you can BLESS!)

At one point you may ask the keyboard, flute, guitar, backup singers, or all of the above to join in together. You may even find yourself asking the congregation to begin singing words to a set pattern. There is one pattern, "Glory come down (x3) Go all around" that burst forth in one service that I often use as HE leads.

Jewish tradition teaches us that the SHOFAR blower should be someone who is admired in the community, a person who is well-liked and one who does good deeds.

If your motive for blowing in any situation is secretly, "I'll show them... God will get them now... they'll be sorry they messed with me!" - then DON'T BLOW. Get your heart right (that a curse will not boomerang on you) and minister in love - for love faileth not - even when we make a mistake.

Don't let ANYONE talk you into blowing if you are uncomfortable with the present circumstances. You can politely say, "I don't believe the timing is right, or I'm not sure God would approve in this instance."

Remember you are a guest under the authority of your host. Even if you have been promised that you can share and the persons in charge change their minds, don't be offended. It's all in HIS timing. There will be other opportunities and you certainly don't want to disrupt the flow of the Holy Spirit.

GOING FROM FROZEN TO CHOSEN

Always remember that you probably know more about the SHOFAR than any audience you'll stand before because you have taken time to read this book and hopefully done research on your own. Since the original signals were claimed to be destroyed almost 2,000 years ago, there is no right and wrong way to play. You must only please ABBA, Father. If you plan to play one note and another one comes out, transition back to what you want to play. No one will know the difference (unless they read this section of the book and figure it out!! ha, ha). The first sounds of a baby are the most precious to its parents. Therefore, don't say, "This is not good enough!" Do strive for perfection through regimental practice. Practicing two or three times a month will not keep your lip muscles working properly.

BE SET FREE TO MINISTER
Spend time with the giver of all gifts.

John 15:26 "But the Comforter, which is the Holy Ghost, whom the Father will send in my name, He shall show you all things, and bring all things to your remembrance, whatsoever I have said unto you."

2 Corinthians 10:12 "For we dare not make ourselves of the number, or compare ourselves with some that commend themselves: but they measuring themselves by themselves, and comparing themselves among themselves, are not wise."

NEVER, I say NEVER compare your blowing with another. Your experiences from the time you were born will have an influence on what comes forward in the spirit realm through your breath. Only

your unique sound can be a holy experience to certain persons - **it's a spirit-to-spirit ministry**. Everyone has people that only they can reach. God has chosen YOU for a certain anointing - find out what it is and stay with it. HE will expand it when HIS timing is right. In other words, you are not called to be the same as another. Have you ever heard the phrase said, "If two people are exactly alike, then one of you is unnecessary?"

WOULD YOU LIKE TO KNOW HOW TO EMBARRASS YOURSELF?

WHEN IT IS TIME TO SIT DOWN - DON'T SIT DOWN!!!

There are times I'm enjoying fellowship with the Lord and want so much to keep blessing the people that I fail to be aware that it's time to quit. I think, just one more note. Have you ever said to yourself - just one last bite of food and that is the very bite you splatter all over your outfit? Well, the extra note you "splatter" will be remembered more than ALL those you did right, so when it's time to quit - **QUIT!**

HOW TO QUENCH THE MINISTRY
or how to escape the blessings of God!

Put popularity before obedience.

Avoid any thing controversial when you know God has ordained it. "But they might not like it, they may not understand or laugh at me!" If they do snicker and you did blow it (pardon the pun) learn to laugh at yourself

- He who can laugh at himself will never cease to be amused!!!

Sidestep the issues - stop beating around the bush - "beat the bush." If someone isn't offended then you are in the wrong crowd, because the SHOFAR will not only stir up the gifts in people, it will arouse the dormant evil in them also.

Fail to be submissive to the prophet - submit yourself to the leaders in authority and to the house rules!!! You can go later and confront. The service is not the place to do that. You might get in the flesh and close the door forever to not only yourself but to other SHOFAR players in the future.

Judge those around you - People have a tendency to classify everyone together - like a bad employee reflects on the whole business/ ministry. Is someone rude, harsh, uncontrollable; did you see them gossip, curse, drink, act inappropriately? Don't you begin to think, "What is wrong with THESE people" instead of wondering about the individual culprit?

If you begin to fall, let the divine assistance of the Holy Spirit steady you. Romans 3:23 says we have all sinned and fallen short of the glory of the Lord. We will make mistakes but remember that God has a permanent eraser if we'll allow him to use it (this is called repentance!!!). Strive to have a ministry of excellence.

USHER IN THE HOLY SPIRIT

Don't play anything distracting from the assembly. Consider the flow of the service unless God instructs you to change course – The Holy Spirit is flexible to be sweet, somber, convicting, dynamic, lively, or militant.

Be aggressive only when you know in your knower that it is from God that you do these things. Handle with care - appropriately and wisely.

Believe in yourself that you are called, anointed, and appointed.

DON'T LET THE CROWD DISTRACT YOU FROM THE CLOUD! "MOVE WITH THE CLOUD NOT THE CROWD." UNKNOWN

We are what God says we are! How dare we say we are something we are not, such as stupid, ugly, not capable, etc. We would be exalting our thoughts above **His** and are basically calling him a liar. (Isaiah 55:8, "for my thoughts are not your thoughts, neither are your ways my ways, saith the Lord").

Be a blessing as well as be blessed. Don't make excuses, apologize, be embarrassed - you know more than anyone else in the audience; give what you can give & leave the results up to God. They won't know the difference if you make what you consider a mistake - God can turn it into blessings for just one person in the audience!

Fools rush in where angels fear to tread! Some might say, "I'm not afraid to go where angels fear to tread" – have you just called yourself a fool? Know the whole scripture word - not just the part you **want** to know.

Don't recite another's SHOFAR pattern unless you know you are anointed to do it or it will fall flat on deaf ears. God wants us to follow His agenda. You might think, "but I want to bless them in this way or that", when He is wanting to go another direction.

Make sure your own spirit is undefiled – there are times I refuse to play if I know my spirit is not in tune with the timing or I've failed my own testing of my spirit. Be careful what you blast into the atmosphere!

See what others are doing and increase your knowledge - the creativity God's placed in them will activate your own creativity.

Acts 2:37, 38 Peter's words convicted them deeply. Think of these blasts as unspoken words, a secret language of the spirit - this is why you must minister in spirit and in truth!!!

BA'AL TEKIAH
(THE SHOFAR BLOWER)
Please consider these suggestions from experience, observation, and things the Lord has taught me.

Don't misrepresent the office of the SHOFAR!!! We might have the tendency to elevate it, take it too seriously, think the SHOFAR is the only answer, or take it too lightly. Learn to leave the results to God. Don't brag - that's when it won't work. We serve a God who won't let us leave Himself out of the equation. Give Him all the glory; remember it is only a tool.

Are you in competition with other SHOFAR blowers? They are not going to reach the people in the same way that you will or even the same people, so each one has differing gifts. Learn to respect it and be fulfilled with the portion that God has specifically given to you! However, don't be ignorant either -

The SHOFAR is a device that is used to transmit something that is felt. It invades the atmosphere. It is nothing in itself - no sacred object, but needs to be treated with respect as in any audio sound equipment or instrument of music. Think of the SHOFAR as a type of public service announcement or instant magnification of what God wants His people to comprehend. Jeremiah 42:6 states, "Whether it is pleasing or displeasing, we will obey the voice of the Lord our God to whom we send you that it may be well with us when we obey the prophet."

Satan reacts violently sometimes to the sound that penetrates his territory. It's a lot like when we find it difficult to tolerate cursing and people speaking continuous negative words - Satan cannot stay where we are praising and using optimistic words.

Satan may be more committed to stop you than you are in playing and ministering. How committed are you? He is after the seed to destroy - if he can intimidate you then no seed will be sown.

WHEN YOU ARE THE
SHOFAR CHAUFFEUR

TAKE BOTTLED WATER and/or LIP MOISTERIZER.
Your mouth and lips will have the tendency to go dry. A good lip balm will provide more flexibility when playing.

IT IS ALWAYS BEST TO HAVE AN ASSISTANT.
It is surprising how many people would like to help you, but it is best to have someone who can help distribute materials and help you carry your horns. Some well meaning people can let them slip out of their hands or crack them against the wall – mine have bruises to prove this point!

USING A GUITAR STRAP WITH CO-ORDINATING SHOE STRINGS OR A CASE FOR YOUR SHOFAR WOULD BE GREAT.
Tie the strings around each end – about 10" from each side and sling over your shoulder with the bell (large end) always pointing towards heaven.

ON THE AIRPLANE - USE WISDOM
Wrap with bubble wrap (so they can see it is not a fire arm). SHOFARS pack nicely in some golf bags or a hard side bag for the luggage compartment. Say simply, "it is a Biblical Instrument" when asked by officials. Check with each available airline before traveling with a shofar - each one has their own rules and Homeland Security has even additional rules.

IN YOUR VEHICLE

Extreme heat will dry your instrument and it is easy for it to bounce around in the trunk or fall off the seat. A large beach towel wrapped around the SHOFAR will help absorb the bumpy travel.

<u>READY, SET, BLOW!!!</u>

Normally you will use two hands spread apart for a double or triple twist horn.

Always have the open large bell of the horn pointed towards heaven.

When the SHOFAR is twisted into position by a master craftsman, they align the mouthpiece with the bell in the upright position.

Stand relaxed (though you will learn to "look" like you are at attention.) Plant your feet securely several inches apart so you will not lose your balance and never lock your knees, cutting off the circulation and causing you to faint. It is traditional to play with your shoes removed and stand close to where the "Word of God" is taught when in church settings.

Position your face looking straight ahead and bring the horn up to your lips thus placing the horn in a natural position in alignment with your body. THEN you can ever so slightly lean your head upwards if you prefer. (You will notice that many of the SHOFAR blowers in Israel hold their heads all the way back.) When leaning your head back, there is a tendency to cut off your air passage and you might not be able to produce a pure tone – it looks good but isn't too functional. Now if you are as flexible as sword swallower and have learned how to keep that air passage open – then go for it!!!

Your body is divided into two hemispheres. If you have played a musical wind instrument, you may be more comfortable placing the mouthpiece in the middle, which uses both sides of your brain to engage the lip muscles. It may be more comfortable for you to use either the right or left side. There is no right or wrong side to use. One position will seem more natural when you draw up the instrument, you might consider using that on a regular basis unless you think you will eventually blow two at a time.

Keep experimenting with positions and sounds that fit YOUR style and personality.

Try buzzing your lips without your mouth on the horn and spitting out the air – much like spitting out a watermelon seed.
Try the middle and both sides separately to determine what is easiest and most natural.

Too much pressure of the mouthpiece on your lips will prevent the needed vibration to make the sound.
Many blowers actually cut their lips by pressing too hard.

Take a large breath or series of breaths and blow through the means of contracting your stomach muscles.

Breathing exercises increase your air capacity. Begin with about an 8 second intake of air – hold for about 3 seconds and then exhale. Keep practicing until it feels natural. Now you are ready for the big breaths! Take a breath that feels like you are sucking your toes inside out. That is your FIRST breath – hold – breathe a second time - hold it, and then take a third breath on top of the other two!!! You are now ready to slowly release a steady flow into the horn. Refrain from filling up your cheeks and blowing from them. Release the air pressure a little at a time. You can try practicing with those long skinny balloons – stretch it out and blow with an even amount of pressure. You will discover the SHOFAR is much easier to blow when your breathing technique is perfected. See how long you can blow before expelling all the air. (It is reported some SHOFAR blowers can blow over 1 minute without taking a breath).

Hint: You will notice your rib cage will increase. You might consider wearing slightly loose clothing – how embarrassing it would be to split a seam as well as a note!!!

Stretch your lips slightly and increase your breath flow for a higher pitch.
The higher the note, the tighter your tummy.

It normally takes much practice to make the "fog horn" low note.
Completely relax your lower lip and barely put your mouth on the mouthpiece. At times I flutter my tongue to make a unique sound.

HUNTING A HORN

What kind of horn should you buy?

How much do you want to spend? - Horns range in size and shape from $35 to around $600. The Internet and Israel are full of "bargains", but beware – you usually get what you pay for! There are many more bad horns that produce poor tones than are what we consider "clean".

What will be the main usage? - Will you use it for:

Personal warfare - a small ram's horn will do –

Ministering - I suggest one of the larger, more melodic ones – for church, any size will set the enemy to flee – if you are short on funds, at least have a small one to blow before the service to warn the enemy you mean business with God.

Sitting on a shelf – there are some beautiful decorated ones you can purchase – decorated with gold, silver, or leather wrappings, however: they are not necessarily considered kosher by biblical terms and most of them have very poor tone quality.

Who are you purchasing it for? Are you buying it for yourself or the church or another party? Be considerate of what they would prefer and ALWAYS ask the Holy Spirit to direct you.

What size & shape will you want? The small SHOFARS will fit very nice in a coat pocket or purse. For this reason, I suggest you have at least one small one. I use mine in traffic and blow blessings down the highway. I've also used it at night when I sensed danger. Some women carry a whistle but I carry a much more powerful weapon!!! If I'm too scared or tense to blow it, I can always bop someone over the head! My friend says one of his SHOFARS can dent 12-gauge steel.

Sizes vary - to measure the size use a tape measure along the rib or rounded ridge of the horn.

Horn Hygiene

The offensive odor coming from your SHOFAR is due to the flesh that has remained and is continuing to die. Sometimes we stink for the same reason! When you blow through it, your saliva will eventually form a coating on the inside that needs to be purified.

There are various ways to clean your instrument.

Close off small end – use tape or those rubber finger devises purchased at an office supply or drug store.

Fill with deodorant type DRY laundry detergent – use the kind that is perfume and bleach free as not to damage the horn.

Close the large end – a soft flexible ball or a sock works great.

Leave closed for approximately a week.

Empty the contents – a word of caution – DO NOT IMMEDIATELY PUT YOUR MOUTH ON THE HORN AND INHALE – THE RESIDUE WILL BE SUCKED INTO YOUR LUNGS!!! It's also a good idea to make sure you have blown out all the extra soap before you get on stage. I've never blown bubbles, but it might make for an interesting effect!

Use a pipe cleaner or tiny bottlebrush around the mouthpiece – make sure you do not enlarge the opening – this could result in permanent damage to your SHOFAR and may even make it totally impossible to play.

Another method:

Close off small end

Fill with fish gravel – this will remove any remaining flesh.

Close off large end

Shake for 20 to 30 minutes

Empty contents and make sure all the gravel comes out.

Then

Close off the end and pour some people friendly hydrogen peroxide in the horn and let bubble a while or pour in some alcohol and shake back for a few times. I used bleach once and destroyed the beautiful color of my SHOFAR, plus it dried it out. It still played, but I do not recommend using bleach. Alcohol will somewhat dry out the horn, though it does a great job of sterilizing. I store dryer cloths in the bag or in the bell of the horn when not in use.

I carry baby wipes or sterilization wipes if I allow someone to blow my horn to use on the mouthpiece. Seldom do I let anyone blow my special horns used in services. Someone once told me, "Don't allow anyone to blow your horn that you would not be comfortable kissing on the lips!!!"

OIL AS NEEDED

The outside of your SHOFAR will dry and will need to be oiled occasionally to prevent cracking. The finest oil would be some Myrrh from Israel. The next preference would be a fine anointing oil, olive oil (that can become rancid after a long period), and then vegetable oil (which has a tendency to become sticky).

Try to oil your SHOFAR about a week in advance of using it in any public service. The oil makes the horn very heavy and makes playing more difficult. Over-oiling keeps your notes from being so crisp.

Remember that oiling makes the horn slippery and it can slide out of your hand.

I like to use a small amount of cake decorating oil such as peppermint or oil de-mint around the bell (large end) as a fragrance. Avoid using too much for you will choke when you are inhaling a large breath.

And finally, I would like to remind you that we all need to allow the Lord to anoint our head with oil. Be filled with the Spirit and be used as He has called you... and enjoy your SHOFAR journey.

HOMEWORK ASSIGNMENT

WRITE THE VISION Habakkuk 2:2 and make it plain.

Write what you want to accomplish through
your Shofar and document what breakthroughs
you need to accomplish the tasks!!!

Remember to ask the Lord what HE wants you to accomplish -
Jeremiah 33:3 – "Call unto me, and I will answer thee, and
shew thee great and mighty things, which thou knowest not."

BE BLESSED AND SHALOM - PEACE
Meaning nothing missing and nothing broken

PRODUCTS

Shofar Phonetics Volume 1 DVD / Video
One hour of playing, teaching and explaining various sounds and horns.

Shofar Phonetics Volume 2 DVD / Video
30-minute additional sounds and teaching.

Shofar Sow Good
History, specific scriptures, and usage of the Biblical Rams Horn.

Shofar Symposium DVD / Video
One-hour footage from our 2-day workshop with teachings and worship to help evaluate how a workshop at your organization would benefit your group.

www.ShofarPsalmist.org • 214-549-3338

ABOUT THE AUTHOR

Janet Rae Askins began her prayer journey with the Lord when He draped a mantel of supernatural love on her at the tender age of 3 in San Antonio, Texas. Suffering from Mercury and Penicillin poisoning at age 5, her relationship with the Lord further intensified as she laid on a death bed - then with the help of 23 doctors, family support and prayer, she was healed. She later co-owned and operated a business for 20 years, served on several Board of Directors, was President's Ambassador for Lubbock Chamber of Commerce spoke and volunteered in civic and ministry organizations and has been involved in video production. Her passion is to usher people into God's presence so they will discover their lifetime purpose through their true identity in Christ Jesus with the guidance of the Holy Spirit. She authored more than 60 devotionals for Daily Quest, an ESL program, has a booklet, "Shofar Sow Good" and two separate DVD demonstrations titled "Shofar Phonetics". Janet Rae began playing blessings for congregations and TV audiences on the Shofar, a biblical trumpet, in 1997. She has ministered in nursing homes, homeless shelters, and in prisons. Janet Rae is a graduate of Christ For The Nations and has been licensed and ordained by their Fellowship of Ministries and Churches. She is also a certified IFOC Chaplain.

Janet Rae's mission statement is, "to daily discover God's instructions for this season of ministry, using the talents and skills He's given me to be a blessing to and equip others while growing in HIS wisdom and knowledge".

Printed in the United States
By Bookmasters